NOT DISTRACTED

BY

MELVIS MICHAEL

Table of contents

Outline

In this book, Melvis uncovers the multifaceted interruptions we experience in our routine, shows how they keep us from accomplishing our most elevated potential, and offers guidance on the best way to battle against them.

Interruptions can emerge out of our convictions, values, and mentalities, yet they may likewise originate from the local area where we reside and associate. They obliterate our happiness and distance us from God's work. As we pinpoint our interruptions and their sources, we can take ventures toward obstructing them.

Chapter1

Interruptions Bring Unhappiness

In light of interruption, you could trust you have been protected yet some way or another end up in risky circumstances. Frailties, monetary requests, earlier disappointments, and correlations with others are side effects of interruption, and you should know about them. Interruptions influence your bliss. You should hinder what doesn't matter, keep away from schedules that don't uphold your objectives, perceive what's transient, and focus on your family, reason, and confidence. You'll find bliss in things like this. You should look at what invigorates you, what makes you seriously trying, liberal, and caring. Perceive what brings you delight and what causes your interruptions. Try not to stress over being exceptional. People were intended to have various characters that can join as one. More instruction, debates, or interruptions will not improve your confidence. Being unified with others will. Your inheritance will be your undistracted reason and energy and your unselfish love and goal. Different things will show up as interruptions on the other hand.

Chapter 2

Independence from Insecurities

Hard feelings, second thoughts, distress, and misconceptions may all become major interruptions. Individuals frequently construct their penitentiaries. Shame, envy, disdain, and outrage may all detain you. You should track down an organization of individuals who welcome you as you are, which permits you to live without those hindrances.

Everybody is shaky. Try not to disregard weaknesses. Acknowledge them all things considered. Find their starting point and figure out how to dominate feelings that are keeping you down so you can live interruption free.

Chapter 3

Dealing with a Busy Life

Individuals make a normal of 30,000 decisions every day, except not many consider joy in these choices. They get so engrossed with the negative parts of life that they won't ever find euphoria. A great many people look for euphoria at home yet neglect to find it there since they don't keep close by Adequately long. Interruptions like work what're more, arrangements keep them from their cherished ones.

On the off chance that you want a less occupied presence, first, perceive that being unnecessarily occupied is making you despondent. Reconnect with far-off loved ones and give them your undistracted time whenever the situation allows. You should penance for and focus on the individuals you love.

Chapter 4

Discovering Your Life Purpose

Disappointment and difficulties are essential for finding your life's motivation. Try not to rapidly guarantee exploitation. Oppose distress and witness how God utilizes your urgency to bring you effortlessness.

At the point when you live deliberately, blissfully, and without interruptions, you'll quit thinking often about
void social capabilities like riches and
position. Subsequently, interruptions will
become feeble when you fabricate a mindful
gathering around you who will not
dislike your stumbles and who will
feature your true capacity and help you to remember your motivation.

Chapter 5

Carrying on with a Full Life

With God's authorization, you can coordinate your life to any place on the planet. Just the middle is now involved by Jesus. To be capable to travel anyplace you want, you need to transform your thought process. No one is permitted to gatekeep your life and happiness any longer. You should likewise quit mentioning approval to experience what God has placed in your spirit and requested you to release to the universe.

Try not to let commonality or others' assumptions occupy you. Try not to trust that endorsement will follow your objectives and aspirations. Experience God's will.

Chapter 6

Setting Your Waypoints

Long journeys are isolated into more limited waypoints. Momentary focuses let you track your advancement toward a bigger goal.
Consider your life's waypoints a progression of objectives and yearnings. View as significant, near one another achievements that add to a bigger goal.
Individuals who accomplish a ton in life are overflowing
with energy and getting through desires.
They pick a course and embrace the activities important to following it. Be one of them to rediscover bliss.

Chapter 7

Limits and Engagement

Others see your life according to their viewpoint, not yours. A significant number of them reach you continually and feel qualified to give their sentiments on your life. On the off chance that they occupy you or make you despondent, you can decide to overlook them. Put down your stopping points. That being said,
limits are not outright elements. Keep up with
a sensible degree of commitment to
others. On the off chance that you deny all entrance, you will be left
alone and detached.
Many individuals treat their relationship with Jesus in the following way. Following Jesus comprises storing up information in scriptural sections and petitions and disregarding down-to-earth
strict activities. A strict association,
be that as it may, should be reasonable and adjusted.

Chapter 8

Settle on Your Own Choices

Not all realities might become convictions, nor are all convictions realities. While this is generally unharmful, deceptions can be diverting when it comes to confidence and they can hinder your reason. Individuals will quite often adhere to people who think and act indistinguishably from them rather than looking for reality and accepting it. These people groups are among the greatest and most covert interruptions. On the off chance that you need an intentional life, you should make
your own choices about what you accept.
Suppositions about what you ought to think,
the bits of insight you've ignored, and the falsehoods
you've taken from others should be abandoned.
Question is as vital for confidence as activity. It pushes you to look for help. It would be ideal for you to embrace
Jesus in your questions so he can assist you with finding

your way once more.

Chapter 9

Love and Availability

Everyone needs acknowledgment, love, and associations in their lives. Love courses through each individual. Individuals can emphatically impact, what's more, change each other through demonstrations of adoration furthermore, consideration since God gives individuals to one more as opposed to sending them messages. Time, ability, and cash might produce accessibility for the things that matter in your life. Taking out a critical interruption implies turning out to be more open and not squandering your accessibility on it, be it individuals or things. Search for individuals who will be accessible to you, and be accessible for them.

Chapter 10

Words are Powerful

These days, the words individuals use are frequently dastardly and terrible. That's what Jesus says
words are a sign of what lies
in an individual's heart. Words have turned
into hurtful interruptions to individuals and networks.
Your words are a power that can work, as a matter of fact
or on the other hand, annihilate. Pick them reasonably and steer them
from cynicism since they can elevate the individuals locally and push them
towards the best.

Chapter 11

Botches Don't Define You

Try not to allow your disappointments to characterize you as an
individual. Disappointments are an occasion, not a personality.
Regardless of whether you get occupied by your disappointment,
you are as yet adored by God. At that moment when you make a
botch, it fills in as a sign of how much
you want God in your life. Many individuals in history had large disappointments. For example, Walt
Disney lost employment at a paper given
his absence of inventiveness, and Bill Gates' first business was a disappointment.
Relinquish the bias that God doesn't
love you due to your missteps. If you
at any point fizzle, Jesus' penance for humanity will
Make up for you, regardless of anything.

Chapter 12

Legitimacy Builds Connections

To conceal the sting of disappointment is a charming
enticement for the people who have flopped in the past. In any case, you ought to be genuine if you need to move further in your connections. Unselfishness is the principal way to turn into more bona fide. If you will have
solid connections, you must tell the truth
what's more, striking.
Being transparent about the bits of insight and points of interest in your own life are one more approach to
turn out to be more legitimate. Coming clean is the most effective way to dispose of interruptions and
construct trust.

Chapter 13

Embrace Disappointments

Disillusionments can turn into an interruption, however, you can stay away from that by changing
them into a growth opportunity that energizes assurance as opposed to harping on the
the injustice of life. Frustrations are
often grand redirections. God is never overwhelmed since He knows unequivocally what He is doing.
Moreover, you are not a casualty of dissatisfaction. Frustration
shows that you are precisely the exact thing God needs
you to be: a member throughout everyday life. God is
transcendent and consequently, you should
quit figuring you can have command over all parts of your life since that will prompt frustration. Utilize God's shocks as fuel
for activity and obligation.

Chapter 14

Get back to your root

Some of the time surrendering ideal pursuits could appear to be purposeless or unattainable and go back to your foundations. Getting back to roots isn't about revoking your fantasies but being more certain about how God made you. It infers resting and recuperating rather than pursuing impossible objectives.

Additionally, don't agree with what's accessible if you need to intentionally live. Zero in on your starting points and on what you consider significant rather because that is where you will find your fantasy life.

For a truly satisfying life, you should know the the complete truth about your personality and your way. The difficulty is that you frequently don't have

a say in what you understand to be true regarding yourself, and
it is rather forced on you by your loved ones, companions, and the local area.
Interruptions emerge from the accounts you tell yourself, and you wind up making rules to keep up with these accounts set up.
Reevaluate these standards every once in a while to see whether they are keeping you from your objectives, in which case you want to let them go.

Chapter 15

Let People Go

As indicated by the standard of Occam's razor, the least demanding clarification is presumably right.
Consider the least difficult clarification instead of
getting occupied by the many subtleties twirling around in your mind. Frequently, individuals will
get you wrong. This doesn't intend that
you are the issue. Review Occam's razor.
The basic clarification is that those individuals try not to grasp you. Try not to allow that to occupy
You will be ceaselessly misjudged
while following Jesus. Your confidence may push individuals to leave you, however, don't let their
takeoff occupy you. Acknowledge it and proceed
following your motivation.

Chapter 16

Work and Identity

Attempting to appear to be significant diverts quite a large number of individuals. God knows and loves you, thusly you're as of now significant. Being unassuming will assist you with keeping away from the interruptions of faking significance. Work is frequently connected to sensations of self-esteem and personality. Interruption-free living requires a superior and better comprehension of your work and the spot God means for it to have in your life.

Work is crucial, yet it could not hope to compare to the significance of your objectives, individuals you support, and the reasons you accomplish the work you do indeed. Stay zeroed in on your motivation and seek after it with power and energy.

Chapter 17

Preparing

Assuming you wish to do God's will, play out the assignment
He has allocated you until it is finished, just
as Jesus did. The last thinking about venturing might require
the help of someone else. Encompass
yourself with people who have
characteristics like persistence and imagination
to drive you forward.
Recognizing your very own interruptions
is the most important phase in settling your concerns also, advancing. Concocting an arrangement to bargain
with interruptions is another fundamental stage
to limiting their harm. Continually
remind yourself and people around you that
you each have fundamental work that requires
to be finished. This is the method for remaining
undistracted and developing a dependable and
vigorous life plan.

About the Author

MELVIS MICHAEL is a pharmacist by profession. She's also a writer. She writes on health related topics as well as other fields. Two of her books include ," why women can't sleep;women's new mental implosion" and " The Fasting path".

www.ingramcontent.com/pod-product-compliance
Lightning Source LLC
LaVergne TN
LVHW052107160826
845678LV00015B/3406

* 9 7 9 8 8 4 6 6 2 9 2 0 2 *